making mindful

magic

mindful experiences for children

written and illustrated by Lea M°Knoulty

National Library of Australia Cataloguing-in-Publication entry
McKnoulty, Lea, author, illustrator
    Making mindful magic
    Mindful activities for children
    ISBN: 9780994255204 (paperback)
    Series: Making mindful children
790.13

Book design by Louise McKnoulty
Production and editing by Katie McKnoulty, The Light Studio
Printed by Tien Wah Press

The font used in this book is Fabula, identified by The Typographic Design for Children Project as being very easy for children to read.

Visit *www.makingmindfulmagic.com* for more mindfulness ideas and copies of this book

dedicated to
my children
Chris, Katie and
Louise

Every day
Every few days
or even once a week
Open this book
Connect with a page
and do it

sit quietly

Why be busy all the time?
Always watching, always reading
always talking, always moving
always doing!
For five minutes sit and do nothing at all
Just be still

follow a bird

Watch a bird at work
He does one thing at a time
He flies
He walks and looks for food
He finds what he needs to make a nest
Birds remember their purpose

walk barefoot on grass

Heavy green grass connects
with soft shoeless feet
Mother Earth meets you here
Go walking together
No need for a place to go

take as long as you can

Why hurry? Must everything be fast?
Is there a prize?
As slowly as you can
walk up stairs
draw a picture
make your bed
The prize is feeling calm

find stars

Night-time falls, darkness comes
Reminders of the world's greatness
twinkle in white above
Cool night air fills lungs
and awakens senses
There is much to love
about finding stars

paint

Brush, paint, paper
Time stands still
There is nothing else
but what you create
It is in the doing
not in the done that matters

watch waves

Nature is in charge here
Backwards and forwards the waves live
Retreat and advance, the story is endless
changeless, timeless
The only stillness is in your mind
The only silence is you

go walking in nature

A track leading somewhere
The somewhere doesn't matter
on-the-way discoveries matter
Wildflowers of colour,
Stones flat, round, jagged
Leaves like stars, soft or shiny, dead brown
or glossy green, pointy or round

do yoga

Legs crossed sitting on the floor
The only sound is breathing, slow and deep
Try starting this way
Each pose holds all your attention
Child's Pose is for feeling calm
Tree Pose is for concentration
Shoulder Stand brings happiness
Corpse Pose is for doing nothing at all
Remember to finish this way

climb a tree

Long limbs, tree trunks
bare legs, barked branches
hair messed, leaves shaking
Arms and legs take turns climbing
Does the world feel different up there?

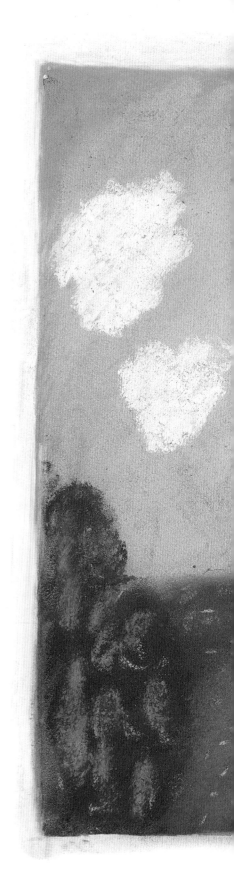

gaze at treetops

Stretched under the biggest,
oldest tree you can find
Looking up to a maze of branches
with leaf fingers
Eyes open wide as visitors come and go
Birds, butterflies, grasshoppers

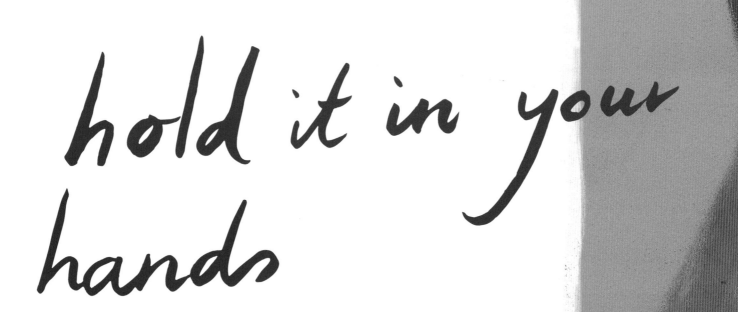

hold it in your hands

Cupped hands hold your attention
Put there something of beauty
Perhaps a leaf
maybe a flower
Let it hold all your attention
Just for a while

why be mindful?

The pages of *Making Mindful Magic* are filled with ideas to help children, or anyone, practice being mindful. To be mindful is to pay attention to the moment you are living right now.

Practicing mindfulness makes us more grounded, brings inner calm and clarity of thought. It encourages us to live authentically and be happy with what we have and who we are. Who wouldn't want to offer these gifts to their children?

You'll find the experiences in this book are mostly free, spent in nature and devoid of technology. They encourage slow, purposeful engagement with the world and the inner self. For many children today there is little time to be alone, to deeply connect with an activity or surroundings.

Making Mindful Magic is a book for doing, to ignite the senses and the imagination, to encourage focused interaction with an experience. Our children deserve to be exposed to mindfulness and its benefits, so they may continue to incorporate and expand upon it for the rest of their lives.

I hope that *Making Mindful Magic* is a place to start this process.

Lea McKnoulty

how to use this book

Any aged child or adult can use this book and enjoy the surprise of randomly opening the book at a page and doing the mindful activity. The amount of adult participation and guidance required will depend on the age of the child. A very young child will enjoy the pictures and verses but can also participate in the activities, with your help. An older child will have the ability to be more independent – they can read and initiate their own practice eventually.

Some suggested ways to interact with *Making Mindful Magic*:

- You can set the scene by noting this time as 'quiet time'.
- Invite calmness by beginning with deep breathing into the lower belly.
- Initially ask your child to flip through the book and imagine doing one of the activities or to find the one they'd like to try.
- Read the verse and take in the picture together, exploring any concepts of interest or that may be new to your child. You could get specific with something like, "What do you think it means when it says…" When looking at the pictures you might like to say something like, "Does the picture make you think of anywhere you know or something you have done before?" Questions like this will help your child focus on engaging with the activity mindfully.
- Ideally your child can be involved in the logistics also. Ask them, "Where will we do this activity?" and "What things will we need to do it?"
- When they are familiar with the idea, a daily random opening of a page is a great practice to adopt.
- Generally speaking, the younger the child the less time you would spend engaging in an activity as their concentration span may not be very long. Many experts recommend one minute for every year in age.
- A bell is a fun way to time the activity.
- The suggested prompts for each activity below ideally are for pre or post experience discussions. The goal is just being in nature or being in the activity. However, depending on your child and particularly at first, you might find it helpful to use the prompts during the activity to help them focus – like the way a guided meditation works for an adult.

Meditation is the ultimate mindful experience and sitting quietly is really a pre-meditation experience that is worth encouraging. Meditation practice brings peace and calm to everyday life and the subsequent reduction in stress levels is well documented.

You could start a discussion by asking, "What do you think might happen if you just sit and do nothing?" or "How do you think it will make you feel to sit quietly?" and "Do you think your body will feel different?" or "Maybe you will hear different sounds?" You can ask them to watch for these things before they begin or remind them during it if they seem distracted or afterwards as a follow-up. You can also experiment if this is best done with eyes open or closed.

follow a bird

Birds in nature are so single-minded, they can teach us so much about being mindful. If a bird is hungry, all it does is look for food. If a bird is building its nest, all it does is collect the materials. By quietly following a bird's activity a child can learn to be purposeful, to act with commitment and to be mindful.

Children must be quiet for this activity and will soon learn if they are noisy, then the bird will fly away; even a young child will work this out quite quickly. Perhaps your older child might enjoy a pre-discussion about predicting what the bird will do and where it will go. It may help with focusing to firstly ask them to simply look at the bird's physical features or listen for any sounds that the bird makes. Post-activity, a discussion about how the bird goes about his business with great purpose may be helpful.

walk barefoot on grass

Walking barefoot on grass is not something new. But to do it with full attention is a new experience for many. Try it yourself and you'll be surprised to feel the difference in your body. You become calmer and feel very connected to the earth and your inner self.

Before you begin the barefoot walk ask your child to think about what they feel in their feet when they connect their bare feet with grass. When they have their shoes on later you could ask them how their feet feel differently now or ask "Did you feel differently in any other way? "

take as long as you can

Multi-tasking is celebrated in our world today, but it isn't a skill to be encouraged in children. Instead you can teach sole-tasking by encouraging your child to try taking a long time to perform a task. No matter the task, the point is to focus mindfully on one activity until it is finished.

Before you begin and after the task, you could ask your child the questions posed in the verse. Start small with something like brushing teeth and build up to something more time consuming like washing up. I appreciate this is difficult in our regular day-to-day lives but by practicing the skill of 'going slow', we teach children the art of focusing and seeing a single task through to the end and allow them to experience the associated satisfaction in doing so and the calmness it brings.

find stars

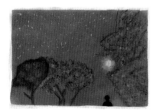

Opportunities for mindfulness are all around us in nature, even at night-time. Your neighbourhood may be doused in city lights so stargazing may require a short drive to open up a whole new experience connecting with nature. Being quiet, focusing attention upwards, not on the ground where we normally look offers a new space for children to engage with.

Before you begin you could talk about looking for patterns in the stars, looking for differences in the brightness of different stars. You could also ask your child to think about how their body feels in the night air. Afterwards you could ask, "Were the stars all shaped the same?" or "Did you notice if there was a moon tonight?" and "What do you remember about the night sky?" or "How did it feel to breathe the night air?" A fun thing to do is to ask your child to make up names for stars and star groupings, maybe they can look for an animal or an object in the night sky.

paint

The thing about painting is it's quite hard to think of anything else while you're doing it! Mindfulness and creating go hand in hand – time flies and purposeful activity flourishes; all you need to do is supply the space and materials.

We don't, as adults, need to judge the artwork or process or ask children to name the things they've created. The point is to create, not to produce a masterpiece and to focus, as the verse states, on the process rather than the product. By exploring the materials and how they can be used, true mindfulness is experienced. The younger the child, the bigger the brush and the larger the piece of paper!

watch waves

Waves crash, water moves back and forth, but your own mind can be very still amongst it all. A sense of deep calm can be summoned in the midst of this wild activity. This is good training to connect to your inner self despite what may be happening around you.

There are concepts from the verse you can discuss with your child. You could suggest things like, "Watch the waves going backwards and forwards" or "Try keeping your mind and body very still while you watch" or "Watch how far the water comes in and goes back out" or "Are the waves all the same as they roll in?" Maybe with older children you could look for an individual wave's life cycle – watch it start, come in and retreat to form another. Listen for the start of the sound and how it changes as the wave comes closer. A post-experience conversation may focus on recalling how they felt as they sat watching all the activity around.

go walking in nature

This is not the same as running around wildly in a park. This is about connecting with nature. It's about mindfully observing all around you, listening to the quiet or the sound of the birds, breathing in the fresh air, smelling its perfumes and feeling it encompass your whole body.

You could put a timeframe on the walk or designate a specific area to walk in. Of course this can happen in your own backyard! Some post-experience discussion could centre on what they observed and how being in nature makes them feel.

do yoga

Children will love the idea of doing yoga. Young bodies are supple and the poses can be done by anyone, at any level. Yoga is non-competitive which means you connect with yourself and your own movement rather than think about who is the fastest or the best. As the verse suggests, it offers the opportunity to be mindful when the poses are done in a quiet place with calmness and purpose.

On our website *www.makingmindfulmagic.com* you will find a simple yoga routine for children or you could just do the poses in the verse. The main things to remember include starting with quiet time, sitting cross-legged, breathing slowly and quietly and ending with the full relaxation pose, corpse-like on the floor. You will know your own child's capabilities depending on age and dexterity.

climb a tree

When well-focused and mindful, tree climbing is a safe retreat for children and of course the largest tree doesn't need to be chosen! It may however be useful to have a pre-experience discussion about how high to go and how long to stay up there! Even a young child will feel high up in the tree if you lift them onto a low hanging branch and hover.

Before climbing, the discussion could be about the need to focus on purposefully moving legs and arms onto branches and grounding themselves there before moving higher; about being mindful of how bark may feel different on hands and feet; of the smells they notice when they are in the tree versus when they are just looking at it; and of course how the world looks from up higher.

gaze at treetops

When we really connect with nature and observe carefully what is around us, we can't help but be mindful. Treetops are full of wonder – things to see, things to hear, things that move, like birds and butterflies and things that don't move like exquisite coloured bark or branches and leaves. It can only be appreciated by being in the moment. If your mind is somewhere else, you miss it all!

Before you begin, ask your child to look out for what is in the tree, perhaps the colours, for what is moving or still. Ask, "Are all the leaves the same?" and "What can you see through the leaves?" The idea is to concentrate on the moment, to be observant and present in a peaceful way.

hold it in your hands

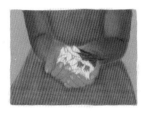

How often do we pick things up thoughtlessly in our hands, allowing the beauty and wonder of what we are holding to go unnoticed? In this experience, encourage your child to find a thing of beauty and to closely observe it in her hands. It really doesn't matter what it is and of course the same activity can be done over and over with different things.
The point is to closely look at the object in a different way – turn it over, look at parts never noticed before. Before beginning you could talk together about looking for the colours, shapes, textures, smells; this is an opportunity to explore the senses. Afterwards you can talk about the discoveries that were made.

Visit *www.makingmindfulmagic.com* for more mindfulness ideas and copies of this book.